TAIZÉ

A COMMUNITY AND WORSHIP:
ECUMENICAL RECONCILIATION
OR AN INTERFAITH DELUSION?

TAIZÉ

A COMMUNITY AND WORSHIP:
ECUMENICAL RECONCILIATION
OR AN INTERFAITH DELUSION?

CHRIS LAWSON

LIGHTHOUSE TRAILS PUBLISHING, INC.
EUREKA, MONTANA

Taizé—A Community and Worship: Ecumenical Reconciliation
or an Interfaith Delusion?
© 2017 Chris Lawson
Lighthouse Trails Publishing, Inc.
P.O. Box 908
Eureka, MT 59917

Library of Congress Cataloging-in-Publication Data

Names: Lawson, Chris (Pastor), author.
Title: Taize : a community of worship: ecumenical reconciliation or an
    interfaith delusion? / Chris Lawson.
Description: Eureka : Lighthouse Trails Publishing, Inc., 2017. |
Includes
    bibliographical references.
Identifiers: LCCN 2017020280 | ISBN 9781942423256 (softbound
: alk. paper)
Subjects: LCSH: Communautbe de Taizbe. | Salvation--Christianity. |
    Salvation--Catholic Church. | Catholic Church--Relations--Prot-
estant
    churches.
Classification: LCC BV4408 .L39 2017 | DDC 271/.8--dc23 LC
record available at https://lccn.loc.gov/2017020280

Note: Lighthouse Trails Publishing books are available at special quantity
discounts. Contact information for publisher in back of book.

DEDICATION

This book is dedicated in love to the untold millions of Christian believers, both young and old, who, in their zeal for ecumenical unity and revival, have somehow missed the words and warnings of the Lord Jesus Christ who said,

"Take heed that no man deceive you." (Matthew 24:4)

Booklets by Chris Lawson

Yoga and Christianity: Are They Compatible?

How to Know if You are Being Spiritually Abused or Deceived—A Spiritual Abuse Questionnaire

The Alpha Course: An Evangelical Contradiction

A Directory of Authors: Three NOT Recommended Lists

Contents

A NOTE TO THE READER

As one of the editors of this book, I was asked if I would write the foreword because I have a very curious history with Taizé in France. No, I have never been there, and what little I knew of it had nearly been forgotten when Chris Lawson's book came across my desk. And yet, in an indirect way, Taizé has had a major impact on my life.

Before I explain all this, let me use an analogy of what transpired. In some ways, my life as a Christian has been like a battleground, but in my younger years, I was never too anxious to fight. Often, I was one of many who stood on the sidelines and just observed. But I've learned that this is not really a safe place to be; and when it comes to Taizé, I got caught in the crossfire.

Yes, I am a casualty to Taizé, but at the time, I did not realize from whence that flaming missile came. After reading this book by Chris, I now understand.

Let me share some memories of what happened. Having been raised Roman Catholic and entering my twenties, I was very familiar with what I would later realize as the bondage of Roman Catholicism—bondage to guilt, bondage to sinful habits and attitudes, but most especially, bondage to a false gospel of salvation (i.e., through participation of sacraments and good works).

When I was drafted into the U.S. Army at twenty years old, I experienced a spiritual crisis, and through meeting a born-again Christian fellow soldier and reading the Bible, I came to understand justification by grace through faith and of being born of God's Spirit. I surrendered my life to the Lord as He captivated my heart and my life.

After this, I had a burning desire to serve the Lord for the rest of my life—in no matter what capacity God called me to. After my time in the service ended, an opportunity arose for me to join a Christian community composed of a group of Christians who served the Lord together. I wanted this because I felt I could serve the Lord better by working with other Christians rather than trying to serve the Lord alone.

I became an integral part of this community after getting to know the elder (second only to the senior elder) and meeting one of the members who had just returned from spending a year in France. He was very excited about his experience; but when he shared with me some of the "insights" he gained while in France, in particular from Taizé Community (notably that doctrine was not important as long as there was unity), I expressed my concern that doctrine should be very important. He seemed offended with this and henceforth always distanced himself from me, but he and the elder I mentioned spent much time together in private discussions.

Fast-forward six years, for I had been with this Christian community for that length of time. The senior elder (who was also the founder) of the community had just been booted out. The other elder called it "discipline," but as it turned out, he was never to come back. The elder, who largely headed up the disciplinary action, told the expelled senior elder he could return after he "repented," but the fact is, our senior elder had nothing to repent of. You see, most of the leadership of the community had secretly conspired that all of us should become Catholic. Since the senior elder would not endorse such a move, they removed him. Eventually, they got rid of me too because I could not in good conscience go back to the Catholic Church.

During this time, a lot of upheaval took place whereby two of the married men were also kicked out of the community; in each case the wife and children stayed behind, and the marriages ended in divorce. The senior pastor (who had been expelled) had a married daughter with children living in the community; he later died with a broken heart because of the estrangement from his daughter and grandchildren. Basically, this community had become cult-like while transforming itself from a loving Christian ministry into a Roman Catholic cloister.

Not long before I left the community, the elder, who had been conferring with the member who had been to France, confided in me that becoming Catholic had been discussed privately years earlier. But the elder had told him and other members, "it's not time yet!" As I read and helped edit this book on Taizé, I realized for the first time that Taizé had been perhaps the biggest catalyst in propelling the community I had once so dearly loved into Catholicism. When I learned that tens of thousands of young people go to Taizé every year, I knew we had no choice but to publish this warning.

DAVID DOMBROWSKI

CHIEF EDITOR AT LIGHTHOUSE TRAILS

TAIZÉ, BURGUNDY, FRANCE

CHAPTER 1

A COMMUNITY IN THE MOUNTAINS OF FRANCE

During World War II in France, a Swiss Reformed Protestant named Roger Louis Schütz-Marsauche began reaching out to suffering people, in particular refugees from the war. Through his efforts, Taizé Community, located in the village of Taizé, Burgundy, France, was birthed. The community website describes Taizé's founder:

> Everything began in 1940 when, at the age of twenty-five, Brother Roger* left Switzerland, the country where he was born, to go and live in France, the country his mother came from. For years he had been ill with tuberculosis, and during that long convalescence he had matured within him the call to create a community. [1]

*The name Roger Louis Schütz-Marsauche eventually came to be affectionately known as by his followers.

The community that "Brother Roger" began has since become an internationally recognized ecumenical monastic brotherhood receiving a hundred thousand visitors each year. The community website describes the early days of Taizé:

> The small village of Taizé, where he settled, was quite close to the demarcation line dividing France in two: it was well situated for sheltering refugees fleeing the war. Friends from Lyon started giving the address of Taizé to people in need of a place of safety.

> Gradually, other young men came to join the original group, and on Easter Day 1949, there were seven men who committed themselves together for their whole lives in celibacy and to a life together in great simplicity.

> In the silence of a long retreat during the winter of 1952-53, the founder of the community wrote the Rule of Taizé, expressing for his brothers "the essential that makes the common life possible."[2]

In 1958, Brother Roger was introduced to Pope John XXIII shortly after he became pope for the purpose of discussing "reconciliation" between Catholics and non-Catholics. Brother Roger described the meeting:

> [Pope John XXIII] showed himself to be very attentive to the question of reconciliation and ended the conversation by asking us to return. That first meeting with the pope communicated to us an unexpected impetus.[3]

The following year, Pope John XXIII invited Brother Roger to participate as an observer in Vatican II, which was to commence in 1962. Renting an apartment in the center of Rome with other brothers from Taizé, Brother Roger attended all but two of the Vatican II meetings over a four-year period. This had a great impact on his life and spiritual outlook in the years to come.

Brother Roger was motivated to help hurting people by creating an atmosphere of love, acceptance, and unity among people of all faiths. However, his passion to help others overrode any desire for biblical discernment, and he neglected to protect and uphold the Gospel message that presents a narrow way to truth, wherein salvation comes only through one Person rather than all paths leading to God.

After serving for many years as a champion for ecumenism and unity between Roman Catholics, Protestants, and Orthodox believers, Brother Roger's life, at the age of ninety, was terminated on August 16, 2005 when he was brutally murdered during an evening service at Taizé by a tormented knife-wielding Romanian woman named Luminiţa Ruxandra Solcan.

Though Brother Roger is gone, his legacy at Taizé lives on, and tens of thousands of mostly young people continue to be strongly influenced by this man's life, beliefs, and teachings, not only in France at the physical location of Taizé but around the world in Taizé worship meetings.

The Taizé Community

RECONCILIATION— "A THEOLOGICAL THEME" AT TAIZÉ

I n a book titled *A Community Called Taizé: A Story of Prayer, Worship, and Reconciliation* (with a foreword by Desmond Tutu), author Jason Brian Santos says that the "three prominent theological themes of Taizé are *reconciliation, freedom* and *trust.*"[1]

In explaining "reconciliation," Santos says that Brother Roger did not want any particular "theology" at Taizé because that would hinder the "reconciliation" between those of different religious persuasions. Santos describes Brother Roger's ecumenical vision:

> As the community developed and new brothers joined Brother Roger, it became apparent that genuine ecumenism would be one of the most significant challenges the community would face. After all, for over *four hundred years estrangement* had existed between Protestants and Catholics. But for the young Swiss theologian, it was four hundred years *too many.* Brother Roger understood *all of humanity to be reconciled to God in and through*

Christ. . . . all are equal in Taizé; the community becomes a living example of reconciliation. . . .

This, to a large degree, is why the Taizé chants were birthed to help bring young people from different Christian traditions together in a unified expression of prayer.[2]

Bearing in mind that these "unified expression[s] of prayer" are largely mystical repetitive chants and other contemplative practices (e.g., lectio divina, centering prayer), the words of the Catholic contemplative monk, Thomas Merton, come to mind. Merton once described a conversation he had with a Sufi (Islamic mystic) leader who told Merton there could be no fellowship between those of different religions as long as doctrines (he referred then to the "doctrine of atonement or the theory of redemption"[3]) stood in the way. Merton assured him that while doctrines such as these were a barrier, there could be unity of spirit *in the mystical realm.*[4] This is what Brother Roger was proposing for Taizé.

Jason Brian Santos, who spent time at Taizé researching the community, sums up Taizé's view of reconciliation:

When Christ made all things new, he restored in us the image of God. Moreover, this image was restored *in all of humanity.* As a consequence, when we see our neighbor *we ought to see the image of God; we ought to see Christ.*[5] (emphasis added)

Webster's Dictionary defines "reconciliation" as "the act of reconciling, or the state of being reconciled; reconcilement; restoration to harmony; renewal of friendship."[6]

To the Catholic Church, this reconciliation means something very different from the idea of two friends reconciling after a disagreement or estrangement. Rather, it sees the "reconciliation" between Catholics and Protestants as the reabsorption of Protestants into the Catholic Church. The Catholic Church, as an institution, has *always* seen Protestants as "the lost brethren," so the only feasible reconciliation is to *bring them back*. The papacy and the Roman hierarchy will only be fully satisfied when they have fully assimilated the Protestant church into *its* system on *its* terms.

In Roger Oakland's book, *The Good Shepherd Calls*, he discusses the "Roman Catholic Ecumenical Delegation for Christian Unity and Reconciliation."[7] Oakland explains the efforts being made by both the Catholic Church and leaders in the Protestant church to eradicate the barriers that keep the Catholics and the Protestants from becoming one church. There is every reason to believe that Taizé desires this very same thing. And with 100,000 people coming to Taizé every year, they very well may see this union take place sooner than later.

An online promotional piece for Jason Brian Santos' book *A Community Called Taizé* by his publisher, InterVarsity Press, asks the question, "Why have millions of young people visited an ecumenical monastic community in France?"[8] Like the emerging-church movement with its sensory-driven mystical contemplative practices, momentum is picking up rapidly in ecumenical movements worldwide. But why has the Taizé Community in particular grown so much in recent years? One apparent answer is that several popes and many Protestant groups have heartily promoted and endorsed it. While it is being touted as a place of reconciliation through love, certainly there is more going on than meets the eye.

BROTHER ROGER (ON LEFT) WITH CATHOLIC AND
PROTESTANT CLERGY, LEAVING AN ECUMENICAL SERVICE
IN ST. STEPHEN'S CATHEDRAL, VIENNA, C. 1975

CHAPTER 3

THE TAIZÉ COMMUNITY IN ECUMENICAL OVERDRIVE

ECUMENICAL ASSIMILATION

Current ecumenical and interfaith movements are expanding like never before. These spiritual trends, and the many Christian denominations and religions involved, are proof that a vast global phenomenon is occurring.

Indeed, a "new spirituality" pushing for global unity and oneness is well underway. Trumpeting unity, peace, and prayer, with key ecumenical and interfaith leaders at the forefront, monks from France's Taizé Community (and a vast array of their young followers) are part of the ever-growing push for global ecumenical assimilation. What is leading this Taizé Community spirituality? Just this—it provides a way of uniting members worldwide from Protestant, Roman Catholic, and Orthodox churches, along with the assimilation of anyone else *from any religion at all.**

---

*See page 69.

A "RECONFIGURATION" OF THE
ECUMENICAL MOVEMENT

On October 22, 2005, at the famous Interchurch Center in New York (formerly known as the Protestant Center, 1948), the former General Secretary of the World Council of Churches, Reverend Dr. Samuel Kobia, gave the keynote address titled "Challenges Facing the Ecumenical Movement in the 21st Century," discussing an ecumenical concept he termed, "mapping the Oikoumene."* Addressing his audience with deep conviction, Kobia encouraged his ecumenical and interfaith followers to be "open to a wide range of possible developments in the 'reconfiguration of the ecumenical movement.'"[1]

Kobia's address further opened the door to the spiritual delusion being embraced by ecumenists and interfaith proponents alike. Kobia stated:

> The ecumenical movement, so long as it remains true to its calling, bringing the whole gospel to the whole world on behalf of the whole church, will prosper through God's grace. . . . we who labor in various ecumenical institutions are

---

*"The word oikoumene, from which the term 'ecumenical' derives, means 'the whole inhabited earth.' In the original Greek, it reflected the interaction of religion, philosophy and political administration as they shaped society. When the New Testament reports an imperial decree that 'all the world' should undergo a census (Luke 2:1), the reference is to oikoumene. In modern usage, the word embraces the unity of God's whole creation and recognizes every human pursuit as subject to the healing ministry of Christ's Spirit."[2]

freed to exercise discernment as to whether our own agencies remain instruments relevant to the demands of this hour—or if God is calling us onward into *other manifestations of Christian ministry*. The exploration of this question, the analysis of existing relations among churches and ecumenical bodies, the felt need for *new relationships and institutions*—all is part of what we mean by "mapping the Oikoumene" while leaving ourselves open to a *wide range of possible developments* in the "*reconfiguration*" of the ecumenical movement. . . . we have learned the importance of hearing authentic voices speaking for traditions *other than one's own.*[3] (emphasis added)

Kobia spoke of the "urgency of inter-religious dialogue in today's world"[4] and questioned whether the churches can "join in voicing a common 'Christian' position on issues under discussion."[5] He suggested:

The need for consensus on *a wide range of issues*— theological, cultural, pragmatic—is, in my opinion, one of the most convincing arguments in favor of multilateral dialogues among the churches. Bilateral dialogue between pairs of churches or confessions have their place, but they are insufficient in establishing a universal sense of Christian identity.[6] (emphasis added)

Kobia questioned how Christians could "relate to people of other faiths" and said Christians "should be inquiring together as to God's purpose for us in a multi-cultural world characterized by a diversity of faiths."[7] He added that there is an:

> unavoidable necessity of engaging ecumenically in what some call "a broader ecumenism," that of *inter-religious dialogue*, especially in clearing away misconceptions between Christians and Muslims and rediscovering our shared values.[8] (emphasis added)

During another event, Kobia stated:

> [T]o gain the capacity to inspire the world, we need inner strength. Our strength *lies also in our unity.* . . . [our] primary purpose is to call one another to visible *unity in one faith* and *one eucharistic fellowship.*[9] (emphasis added)

The World Council of Churches is not the only Christian organization with such rhetoric and religious (and political) statements as this. Many are talking like this today. The problem, however, is that such statements do not reflect biblical Christianity. When leaders like Kobia promote the global ecumenical movement and its extensive "reconfiguration," anyone from any religious tradition can participate. What is the result? An un-Christian one-world spirituality that uses Christian words and phrases but is *not* biblical Christianity in which the message of Jesus Christ—"I am the way, the truth, and the life"—is the primary focus. Jesus' clear statement, "[N]o man cometh unto the Father but by me" is no longer central in a multi-faith ecumenical body. In other words, it becomes an entity that calls itself Christianity but is actually a conglomeration of all beliefs.*

Regarding this multi-faith ecumenism, for many years the modern ecumenists have sacrificed sound biblical theology for the sake of "negotiations conducted between committees of various denominations."[10] However well-intentioned, dialogue sessions and negotiations are steeped in political and religious "correctness." The destruction of the biblical Gospel is generally the end result.

Unfortunately, ecumenical delusions will continue to absorb the undiscerning as long as leaders fuse Christian denominations and interfaith movements together into one hybridized mass.

The contemplative, experience-driven Taizé Community is a prime example of Kobia's "mapping the Oikoumene" and being "open to a wide range of possible developments."

Leaders of the emerging church movement recognize Taizé's influence upon young people who visit the community in France. Robert Wilson Black, CEO of the emergent social-gospel group, Sojourners, sees Taizé as a vehicle to bring about a great ecumenism:

> [T]eens across the world are still flocking to monks in France to deepen their Christian faith. . . . The Taizé community of brothers *from across Christian traditions*—alongside sisters from a

---

*This is actually in contradiction and opposition to Jesus Christ Himself. While posing itself as "Christianity" and working within the church framework, it is perhaps the most damaging thing that has come to the Christian faith.

Catholic order—host religious thinkers, leaders, practitioners, and especially youth who want to *engage biblically* around issues spanning peace, justice, the arts, service, and Christian practice [e.g., *contemplative prayer*]. . . For American Christians who may be stuck in habits of religious thinking that *promote "all or nothing"* [Heaven or Hell], "left and right" interpretations of the Scriptures, Taizé invites us to sing together and investigate the scriptures from a fresh global perspective.[11] (emphasis added)

One may ask, "How do we know the Taizé Community is truly ecumenical and working to unite Protestant Christians, Roman Catholics, Eastern Orthodox, and many other denominations and religions? We can find some of that answer by examining the current Taizé Community website, which upholds their commitment to follow their founding leader, Brother Roger, whose vision it was to bring together Roman Catholics and Protestant Christians:

> Today, the Taizé Community is made up of over a hundred brothers, Catholics and from various Protestant backgrounds, coming from around thirty nations. . . . the community is a "parable of community" that wants its life to be a sign of reconciliation between divided Christians and between separated peoples . . .

> Over the years, young adults have been coming to Taizé in ever greater numbers . . . Sisters of Saint Andrew, an international Catholic community

founded seven centuries ago, Polish Ursuline Sisters and Sisters of St Vincent de Paul take on some of the tasks involved in welcoming the young people.

. . . The community has thus welcomed Pope John Paul II, four Archbishops of Canterbury, Orthodox metropolitans, the fourteen Lutheran bishops of Sweden, and countless pastors from all over the world.[12]

The site explains that "Brother Alois" is the successor of Brother Roger and is the present Prior of the Community.

Catholic cardinal Walter Kasper (President Emeritus of the Pontifical Council for Promoting Christian Unity) was well acquainted with Brother Roger and the Taizé Community. In a 2008 interview, Cardinal Kasper stated:

As the years passed, the faith of [Brother Roger] was progressively enriched by the patrimony of faith of the Catholic Church. According to his own testimony, it was with reference to the mystery of the Catholic faith that he understood some of the elements of the faith, such as the role of the Virgin Mary in salvation history, the real presence of Christ in the Eucharistic gifts and the apostolic ministry in the Church, including the ministry of unity exercised by the Bishop of Rome. In response to this, the Catholic Church had accepted that he take communion at the Eucharist, as he did every morning in the large church at Taizé. . . .

[Brother Roger] described his own personal journey and his Christian identity with these words: "I have found my own Christian identity by reconciling within myself the faith of my origins with the Mystery of the Catholic faith."[13]

In that same interview, Cardinal Kasper described the relationship between Brother Roger and the Catholic papacy:

Every time I met Brother Roger, he spoke to me a lot about his friendship for Pope John XXIII first of all, then for Pope Paul VI and Pope John Paul II. It was always with gratitude and a great joy that he told me about the many meetings and conversations he had with them over the years. . . . the prior of Taizé felt very close to the Bishops of Rome in their concern to lead the Church of Christ along the ways of spiritual renewal, of unity between Christians . . . he felt deeply understood and supported by them in his own spiritual journey and in the orientation that the young Taizé Community was taking. The awareness of acting in harmony with the thought of the Bishop of Rome was for him a kind of compass in all his actions. He never would have undertaken an initiative that he knew was against the opinion or the will of the Bishop of Rome. A similar relationship of trust continues today with Pope Benedict XVI, who spoke very touching words when the founder of Taizé died, and who receives Brother Alois every year in a private audience.[14]

A LIFELONG COMMITMENT TO CELIBACY

One of the primary characteristics of the all-male Taizé Community is the vow of celibacy that each Taizé Community monk commits to—for life. The Taizé website has published the complete vow, beginning with the following text:

> After a time of preparation, a new brother in the Taizé Community makes his lifelong commitment. Here are the words used to express this commitment. . . .
>
> Will you, in order to be more available to serve with your brothers, and in order to give yourself in undivided love to Christ, remain celibate?
>
> I will.[1]

This vow of celibacy required of the "brothers" in the Taizé Community is the same type of commitment required by Buddhist, Hindu, and Roman Catholic priests and nuns. While the vow of celibacy that these community members commit themselves to may appear pious and spiritual, the Bible does not require one to remain single and "celibate" in order to serve God and receive His blessings. Not only that, it can put one into a harmful snare that can lead to much destruction as the Bible warns.

Researcher and author Mike Oppenheimer presents one serious concern with this requirement of celibacy:

Why is there sexual immorality in a church? Very often it is because someone who burns with passion needs to be married. Paul answers this in 1 Corinthians 7:2-3: "Nevertheless, to *avoid* fornication, let every man have his own wife, and let every woman have her own husband. Let the husband render unto the wife due benevolence: and likewise also the wife unto the husband."

Look at what has happened when priests are frustrated in something God commands is good. Because they have forbidden the priests to marry, the Catholic Church has a high percentage of improper sexual conduct, including sexual molestation of children. This is not to impugn specifically the Roman Catholic Church. There are other churches and groups as well that forbid people to marry and make men or women remain single when they are unable to successfully do so.

In the Bible, the qualifications of a priest or bishop do not forbid being married. The Greek word for bishop is *episkopos* and is translated in different Bibles using the same word as elder, presbyter, bishop, [or] priest. Titus 1:5-6 instructs these men to be married and to raise godly children.[2]

This is not to say that sexual molestation (especially of children) only takes place in groups that do not allow/ encourage heterosexual marriage. We know that allowing heterosexual marriage does not per se solve the issue of abuse. For example, Frank Houston (a leader of the predecessor group to Hillsong in Australia) was married but was known to have sexually molested children.[3]

Sadly, the brothers of Taizé willingly restrict themselves from a lifetime of marital intimacy, blessing, and procreation. God's Word speaks very clearly about the origin and practice of "the forbidding of marriage":

> Now the Spirit speaketh expressly, that in the latter times some shall depart from the faith, giving heed to seducing spirits, and doctrines of devils [demons]; Speaking lies in hypocrisy; having their conscience seared with a hot iron; *Forbidding to marry,* and commanding to abstain from meats, which God hath created to be received with thanksgiving of them which believe and know the truth. For every creature of God is good, and nothing to be refused, if it be received with thanksgiving: For it is sanctified by the word of God and prayer. (1 Timothy 4:1-5; emphasis added)

Further implications of Taizé's vow of celibacy can include the hundreds of thousands of young people who come to the community and witness this unbiblical practice. How many have desired to follow in the Taizé brothers' footsteps only later to find themselves in situations that bring them shame and disgrace because they could not live a life where God had never called them?

"GOD LIVES WITHIN EVERY HUMAN BEING"

U tilizing the Taizé Community's ecumenical prayer sanctum as a launching platform to embrace and absorb interfaith, mystical, and ecumenical followers from around the globe, Brother Roger's successor, Brother Alois, states:

> As we continue the pilgrimage of trust on earth that brings together young people from many countries, we understand more and more deeply this reality: all humanity forms a single family and *God lives within every human being without exception.*[1] (emphasis added)

The statement "God lives within every human being without exception" is strikingly similar to a quote Brother Roger wrote attributing the quote to the Vatican II Council when he was attending those meetings in the 1960s. In his 2001 book *God is Love Alone*, Brother Roger relays the incident:

A luminous Gospel insight reappeared during the Second Vatican Council. For a long time it had remained buried under the dust of the ages: "Christ is united to every human being without exception. . . ." Later on, Pope John Paul II would add: ". . . even if he or she is not aware of it."[2]

The 1994 *Catechism of the Catholic Church*, which is the official source for all Roman Catholic doctrine today, further states:

Let us rejoice then and give thanks that we have become not only Christians, *but Christ himself.* Do you understand and grasp, brethren, God's grace toward us? Marvel and rejoice: *we have become Christ.* (#795)[3] (emphasis added)

For the Son of God became man so that *we might become God.* (#460)[4] (emphasis added)

Brother Roger acknowledged in *God is Love Alone* how much Pope John Paul II's words that Christ was "united to every human being" influenced him. He explained that "God remains in communion with everyone."[5]

This belief that God lives in every human being is a New Age panentheistic outlook that has been welcomed not only into the Roman Catholic Church but into many areas of the Protestant church as well. A view also held by both Brother Roger and Brother Alois, it is the antithesis of what the Bible teaches. Furthermore, it is similar to the lie with which Lucifer deceived Eve in the Garden of Eden—"ye shall be as gods."

As we see in Scripture, Lucifer—called the shining one—tempted and deceived Eve, thereby leading her to rebel against God's command to not partake of the forbidden fruit. Through Eve's desire to attain the "knowledge of good and evil," she sinned. The Luciferian bait foisted upon Eve worked, and she partook of the lie, "Ye shall not surely die . . . your eyes shall be opened, and ye shall be as gods, knowing good and evil" (Genesis 3:4-5).

Adam and Eve's selfish and catastrophic moment of sinning "as gods" came about as they disregarded God's command (see Genesis 2:16-17; 3:4-13).

Here is what we need to understand: If God lives within every human being, as the Catholic Church and Taizé leaders declare, then there would be no need for a Savior or for the Cross. Man would already be divine. New Agers believe that God or divinity is in every person and thus do not believe man is sinful nor that he needs a Savior. This type of thinking led New Age author Neale Donald Walsch to say in one of his popular *Conversations with God* books that even Hitler will be in Heaven because there is no sin, there is no evil and no right or wrong.[6] If God is *in* every human being, then this would be true—God was in Hitler.* However, we know that such twisted thinking is absolutely cruel and absurd. While man is made in the image of God (which gives man worth), as a created being, he is not in the same category as God; furthermore, that image is marred by sin.

In John 3, during the discourse between Jesus and Nicodemus, Jesus told Nicodemus, "Ye must be born again"

---

*Neale Donald Walsch went so far as to say Hitler "didn't inflict suffering [on the Jews], he ended it."[7]

to enter the kingdom of God. If God was already in every human being, there would have been no reason for Jesus to say this to Nicodemus. He made the distinction clear, and it was dependent on believing on Him.

Satan is the father of lies (John 8:44) and has always tried to convince man that he is equal to God and does not need a Savior. What better way to send people to Hell than to convince man that God is already in everyone, and nothing else needs to take place? In Warren B. Smith's booklet titled *Be Still and Know That You are Not God!*, Smith states:

> Our Spiritual Adversary would have everyone believe that we are all "one" because God is "in" everyone and everything. . . . To underscore this heretical New Age doctrine of God and Christ "in" everyone, he would have us further believe that nothing of any significance happened on the Cross of Calvary. However, the Bible makes it very clear that something extremely wonderful and overwhelmingly significant did happen on the Cross of Calvary. For it was on that Cross that Jesus Christ died to save the world as He defeated sin (1 John 2:2), death (2 Timothy 1:10), and the Devil himself (Hebrews 2:14).[8]

Taizé leaders have disregarded God's precious Word, and in doing so negated the Gospel message. They have convoluted the will of God through their declaration that "God lives within every human being without exception."

TAIZÉ WORSHIP

The worship practiced at Taizé has attracted many people from around the globe and from many different denominations. While many of the words found in Taizé worship music are words found in Scripture or words that do not necessarily contradict Scripture, the Taizé songs and worship services themselves are centered around contemplative, ecumenical, and oftentimes emergent spirituality themes. The emphasis is not on the teaching or exhortation of the Word of God but rather is to help participants "experience" God through sensory-focused music and singing. A church association in the UK describes the Taizé worship style as such:

> The contemplative worship practices of the Taizé community are promoted at an annual international conference. Taizé worship is being incorporated in a wide variety of churches, both Protestant and Catholic and its pattern of devotion is emulated in other monastic communities around the world.

A WORSHIP SERVICE AT TAIZÉ

A Taizé worship service involves sung and chanted prayers, meditation, a period of silence, liturgical readings, and use of candles. There is no preaching. The style of prayer practiced at Taizé has attracted many worshippers from around the globe and from many different denominations.[1]

The main focus on the Taizé worship is the chanted prayers, meditations, and songs. However, the Bible warns against such practices:

> [W]hen ye pray, use not vain repetitions, as the heathen do: for they think that they shall be heard for their much speaking. Be not ye therefore like unto them: for your Father knoweth what things ye have need of, before ye ask him. (Matthew 6:7-8)

The Contemplative Network, an online resource for those interested in meditative prayer practices, describes Taizé worship and prayer like this:

> For those familiar with Taizé common prayer, but unfamiliar with Centering Prayer practices, they will discover that they *grow from the same root* of seeking to surrender the mind and heart to the intimate presence of God. They *share the same spirit* of ancient monastic traditions to open space to let the Word of God reverberate in all its dimensions. Those who have tasted of this open space during the silent period of a Taizé common prayer service may find themselves *well disposed to explore related*

*contemplative practices such as Lectio Divina and
Centering Prayer.²* (emphasis added)

The Taizé worship is not based on the objective Word
of God but rather offers spiritual experiences that are
subjectively appealing to the flesh. In Scripture, we are
instructed to build up the inner spiritual man and to resist
the carnality of the flesh (Ephesians 3:16, Romans 8:1-16).

> ANYTIME EXPERIENCE IS GIVEN
> HIGHER REGARD THAN GOD'S
> WORD, IT PUTS FOLLOWERS
> AT RISK OF BECOMING VICTIM
> TO DECEPTION AND EVEN
> DANGEROUS SPIRITUAL REALMS.

Jesus Christ instructed His disciples that they should
not use repetitive prayers (chanting) like the heathen (New
Agers, pagans, etc.) do. Anytime experience is given higher
regard than God's Word, it puts followers at risk of becoming
victim to deception and even dangerous spiritual realms.
Mystical and esoteric experiences are subjective, meaning
they are not founded on anything solid or concrete. It
is the Word of God (the Bible) that is to be our steering
mechanism through life. Consider these verses that show
the importance of the Word of God. You won't find any
verses giving credence to seeking after mystical experiences:

For the word of God is quick, and powerful, and sharper than any twoedged sword, piercing even to the dividing asunder of soul and spirit, and of the joints and marrow, and is a discerner of the thoughts and intents of the heart. (Hebrews 4:12)

All scripture is given by inspiration of God, and is profitable for doctrine, for reproof, for correction, for instruction in righteousness: That the man of God may be perfect, throughly furnished unto all good works. (2 Timothy 3:16-17)

Wherewithal shall a young man cleanse his way? by taking heed thereto according to thy word. (Psalm 119:9)

Then said Jesus to those Jews which believed on him, If ye continue in my word, then are ye my disciples indeed; And ye shall know the truth, and the truth shall make you free. (John 8:31-32)

TAIZÉ WORSHIP INFLUENCED BY CATHOLIC PRAYERS

The repetitive Taizé songs are influenced by the Roman Catholic notion that a person needs to say a certain amount of repeated prayers in order for them to be enough (e.g., the Catholic works mentality—which dictates that one must do enough works to reduce the time in Purgatory).

An example in Roman Catholicism would be the Rosary—a droning repetition of the same set of prayers, something like this: six repetitions of Our Father, fifty repetitions of the Hail Marys, and three repetitions of the

Glory-be prayers. These repetitive prayers are usually said before or after mid-week Masses.

Jesus said, when asked about how to pray, to only pray to God (not Mary or saints or angels) and to not repeat the same prayers over and over again like the pagans "for they think they shall be heard for their much speaking."

Six different Psalms tell us to *sing* a *new* song unto the Lord, but not one tells us to chant. Now Psalm 136 is unique in that it uses the refrain "his mercy endureth for ever," but this is not a chant in that each refrain is a response to a different statement. So, unlike the psalms, the Catholic uses endless repetition out of guilt (in doing penance) or to be heard by God or from the sense that the Taizé songs are sung to allow participants to go into mind-altering trance-like states.

TAIZÉ WORSHIP PRACTICES SIMILAR TO NEW AGE MEDITATION

Sadly, many of the spiritual experiences occurring during Taizé worship services are similar to what takes place during New Age meditation. The following quote is from Lacy Clark Ellman, author of the New Age website, A Sacred Journey. Her quote is from "Inside the Taizé Community: An Interview with Brother Emile." The processes (i.e., techniques) she mentions are reminiscent of many transformative occult practices. Regarding Taizé worship, Ellman explains:

> Singing their [Taizé monks] *chants left me transported—centering me*, bringing me peace, and thus *opening me up to the Sacred*. I've been known to describe it as the perfect combination of the *contemplative* and *charismatic*—the words simple

and liturgical in nature, with the repetition making space for the Sacred Guide to enter. . . .

Instead of trying to facilitate an experience with bright lights and catchy songs, the [Taizé] brothers invite visitors into their *own experience—a rhythmic practice of chants, reading, and [meditative] silence* in languages found across the globe. They didn't explain what was going on or how to participate, apart from a board that displayed which song was to be sung next.[3] (emphasis added)

The problem with this explanation is that occultists (shamans, sorcerers, witches, etc.) and New Age practitioners around the globe are receiving similar experiences, in varying forms, through spirit contact via spiritualism, séances, channeling, etc. So too, non-Christians enter varying levels of voluntary and involuntary possession states using this same process.

Instead of encouraging Christian worship settings that provide for a clear understanding of sound biblical preaching and teaching of the Bible, Taizé worship services provide a fast track to spiritual experience via unbiblical forms of prayer, meditation, and silence. In many cases, they bypass the Bible altogether. In settings like this where anything goes—chanting, centering down to enter "the silence," lengthy repetitive singing, and meditative/altered states—any form of spirit contact can occur.

Considering these things, it is of utmost importance that Christians heed this biblical warning:

> Now the Spirit speaketh expressly, that in the latter times some shall depart from the faith, giving heed to seducing spirits, and doctrines of devils. (1 Timothy 4:1)

When people are not being taught the Bible and warned about the dangers of false doctrine and non-biblical practices, they will inevitably, in mystical Taizé type settings, end up under the influence of deceiving spirits. As the above passage describes, strong delusion will overtake them. This is no small problem as it is running rampant in the church throughout the world.

The true Christian has only one option at this point, and that is to obey Scripture and separate from those who bring teachings contrary to the Word of God.

> Now I beseech you, brethren, mark them which cause divisions and offences *contrary to the doctrine which ye have learned*; and avoid them. For they that are such serve not our Lord Jesus Christ, but their own belly; and by good words and fair speeches deceive the hearts of the simple. (Romans 16:17-18; emphasis added)

BIBLICAL UNITY VERSUS ECUMENICAL UNITY

Today, multitudes of professing Christians downplay God's Word in order to experience "unity" at all costs. The unity being implemented rejects biblical separation from false teachers and clings to virtually any belief system as long as the mainstay is unity. But as far as the Bible is concerned, this is not true unity at all. Nor is this unity truly loving, like so many of its followers claim it to be. Contrary to ecumenical unity, biblical unity and love begins and ends with sound doctrine. Sound doctrine is the framework of the Christian faith. Consider the following passage:

> And he gave some, apostles; and some, prophets; and some, evangelists; and some, pastors and teachers; *For the perfecting of the saints,* for the work of the ministry, for the edifying of the body of Christ: *Till we all come in the unity of the faith, and of the knowledge of the Son of God*, unto a perfect man, unto the measure of the stature of the fulness of Christ: That we *henceforth be no*

*more children, tossed to and fro, and carried about
with every wind of doctrine,* by the sleight of men,
and cunning craftiness, whereby they lie in wait to
deceive; *But speaking the truth in love,* may grow
up into him in all things, which is the head, even
Christ. (Ephesians 4:11-15; emphasis added)

Notice in the above text why God gave the offices to
His church—"For the perfecting of the saints . . . Till we all
come in the unity of the faith." Note also that God's desire
is for His people to mature to the point of being "no more
children, tossed to and fro, and carried about with every
wind of [false] doctrine."

We know that Jesus said He would build His church upon
Peter's declaration that Jesus "is the Christ, the Son of the living
God." Jesus stated He would build His church on the bedrock
of this confession:

When Jesus came into the coasts of Caesarea
Philippi, he asked his disciples, saying, *Whom do
men say that I the Son of man am?* And they said,
Some say that thou art John the Baptist: some, Elias;
and others, Jeremias, or one of the prophets. He
saith unto them, *But whom say ye that I am?* And
Simon Peter answered and said, Thou art the Christ,
the Son of the living God. And Jesus answered and
said unto him, Blessed art thou, Simon Barjona:
for flesh and blood hath not revealed it unto thee,
but my Father which is in heaven. And I say also
unto thee, That thou art Peter [Petros = piece of
rock], and upon this rock [petra = mass of rock] I

will build my church; and the gates of hell shall not prevail against it. (Matthew 16:13-18)

It is vital to recognize the importance of the Gospel in this passage—that it is the foundation upon which the church is built. Peter was one of many who strove to build the church on that foundation. But today, where the importance of sound doctrine is undermined, many churches are teetering on a shaky foundation, where the speculations of men are replacing the truth of Scripture.

So too, our Lord Jesus Christ warned His disciples about the spiritual deception of the last days:

> And as he sat upon the mount of Olives, the disciples came unto him privately, saying, Tell us, when shall these things be? and what shall be the sign of thy coming, and of the end of the world? And Jesus answered and said unto them, Take heed that no man deceive you. For many shall come in my name, saying, I am Christ; and shall deceive many. (Matthew 24:3-5)

This period will manifest itself in the form of mass deception—a worldwide delusion precipitated by false prophets and false teachers and culminating with the reign of the Antichrist performing lying signs and wonders (Matthew 24:11-27; see also 2 Thessalonians 2:3, 8-11, Revelation 13). Many of these false teachers even today claim to be Christ or little messiahs, or that "God is in all human beings, without exception" (Brother Alois, Taizé Community), or that they or we are God (or gods) on earth.

Today, more than ever, there are countless tares among the wheat. The Taizé Community and similar ecumenical institutions are helping to bring to fruition an apostate Christianity (whether they realize it or not) that will ultimately draw together a global religious body that will incorporate all religions and in so doing, remove the essence of Jesus Christ's mission when He came to this earth—to proclaim the good news that He is the way, the truth, and the life and that there is salvation in no other name than His (1 Timothy 2:3-6). While the leaders of this effort will be crying peace, love, and unity, in the eyes of God it will be a rejection of His Son's sacrifice on the Cross as redemption for sin (1 Corinthians 15:1-4). If all the religions are valid and if all paths lead to salvation, then Christ's going to the Cross and rising from the dead would have been in vain (1 Corinthians 15:12-17).

> For the time will come when they will not endure sound doctrine; but after their own lusts shall they heap to themselves teachers, having itching ears; And they shall turn away their ears from the truth, and shall be turned unto fables. (2 Timothy 4:3-4)

TAIZÉ AND THE EUCHARIST—AN INTERSPIRITUAL HYBRID

The exchange with God becomes real for us in prayer: by his Holy Spirit, God comes to dwell within us. By his word *and by the sacraments,* Christ gives himself to us.[1]—Brother Alois (emphasis added)

Christ, the Word made flesh, gives himself to us visibly *in the Sacrament.* Draw strength *from the Eucharist,* the meal of thanksgiving, and do not forget that it is offered to the sick of the People of God. It is there for you, frail and weak as you always are.[2]—Brother Roger (emphasis added)

Similar to the Roman Catholic Church, the Taizé Community invokes a "Jesus" that can be eaten and ingested—"the Body and Blood, together with the Soul and Divinity"[3] during Eucharistic services.

It may be that some reading this book are not familiar with the Eucharist, also referred to as the Blessed Sacrament. The word *Eucharist* has a primary appeal to Roman Catholic

Eucharistic adoration. It's worth noting here that many of the Protestant Reformers were burned at the stake for refusing to accept the Catholic Eucharistic belief.[4]

Father John A. Hardon, S. J. wrote an article in *Soul Magazine* (published by the World Apostolate of Fatima) titled "Holy Eucharist is the Whole Christ." The article states:

> The most fundamental question to ask about the Blessed Sacrament is, "Who is the Holy Eucharist?" And the correct answer is: The Holy Eucharist is Jesus Christ.
>
> There is more behind this answer than many Catholics realize. When the Council of Trent in the sixteenth century defined the meaning of the Eucharist, it declared that "the Body and Blood, together with the Soul and Divinity of our Lord Jesus Christ, and therefore the whole Christ, is truly, really and substantially contained in the sacrament of the Holy Eucharist.[5]

The Catholic Eucharist is not the same as the Protestant communion. Protestants traditionally have followed Scripture that tells us to have communion as an act of *remembrance* of Christ dying on the Cross and pouring out His blood for our sins. In the Catholic tradition, a priest performs what is called *transubstantiation*, which Catholics believe literally transforms the wafer into the actual body of Christ and the wine into His blood though maintaining the "appearance" of bread and wine.

Father Hardon continues:

Shortly after Trent, Pope St. Pius V authorized the publication of the Roman Catechism which built on the Council of Trent and explained its teachings for the pastors of the Church.

Regarding the Real Presence, the pastors were told to explain that "in this sacrament is contained not only the true Body of Christ—and that means everything that goes to make up a true body, such as bones, nerves, and so on—but also Christ whole and entire." Consequently the Eucharist contains Jesus Christ in the fullness of his divinity and the completeness of his humanity.

Jesus is therefore in the Blessed Sacrament "whole and entire: the Soul, the Body and Blood of Christ, with all their component parts. In heaven a complete human nature is united to the divine nature in one . . . person. It is a denial of the faith to suppose that in this sacrament there is anything less."[6]

In essence, according to the Roman Catholic Church, you can literally eat Christ, but only a Catholic priest can perform this transformation of a wafer and wine. Robes, incense, and mystical prayer that bring it all together are intended to be reminiscent of the sacrificial altar of the Old Testament. Oddly, chapters nine and ten of Hebrews are contradicted by this ritual in that these chapters describe Christ's sacrifice as a one-time sacrifice that can never be repeated (Hebrews 9:25-28), and that the repeated sacrifices of a priest can never take away sin (Hebrews 10:10-12).

It is also worth noting that in John 6, Jesus refers to Himself as "the living bread which came down from heaven" (John 6:51). But when He says they must eat His flesh and drink His blood in order to have eternal life (vs. 53), even His disciples murmured saying, "This is an hard saying; who can hear it?" (vs. 60). Interestingly, in response, Jesus never gave them a literal rendering of what He had said; and He couldn't have done so because the partaking of any kind of blood was absolutely forbidden in the Law. Jesus made it clear that not only would He soon return to Heaven (vs. 62) and thereby no longer be physically present, but that He had been using a figure of speech, in that there was no benefit in the literal partaking of flesh (vs. 63). His meaning was spiritual—of the eternal life He would offer to those who would believe in His approaching sacrifice at Calvary. Here are Jesus' exact words which are succinct and clearly understandable of His departure to Heaven in the near future and of His figure of speech:

> What and if ye shall see the Son of man ascend up where he was before? It is the spirit that quickeneth; the flesh profiteth nothing: the words that I speak unto you, they are spirit, and they are life. (John 6:62-63)

Upon examination of John 6, it becomes clear that Jesus never intended for people to be thinking they are literally eating His flesh and drinking His blood during communion but that they are *remembering* a very real event that happened only once—Jesus' death on the Cross for the remission of sins as Peter so aptly testified:

> Then Peter said unto them, Repent, and be baptized
> every one of you in the name of Jesus Christ for the
> remission of sins, and ye shall receive the gift of the
> Holy Ghost. (Acts 2:38)

> To him give all the prophets witness, that through
> his name whosoever believeth in him shall receive
> remission of sins. (Acts 10:43)

The popes, the priesthood, and all who believe in the Roman Catholic doctrine of transubstantiation (Sacrifice of the Mass; "re-presenting Jesus") would have to contend with Paul the apostle were he alive today. Paul refuted any ideas about Jesus contrary to Christ's person, nature, and work.

Not only that, Paul referred to perversions of the biblical Jesus, the Holy Spirit and the true Gospel, as "another Jesus . . . another spirit . . . [and] another gospel" (2 Corinthians 11:4). This "another" that Paul is exposing as a dangerous influence is a different "Jesus, spirit and gospel." It is not merely another of the same kind but rather a substitute Christ, a pseudo-Christ, or what Scripture refers to as an anti-Christ—where "anti" not only means *in opposition to* but *in place of* (i.e., a replacement). It is an unbiblical Jesus—a non-scriptural, heretical idea of Jesus, and a false gospel. In actuality, it is no gospel—no good news, *at all.* It is bad news because it removes the Gospel that saves.

> But I fear, lest by any means, as the serpent beguiled
> Eve through his subtilty, so your minds should be
> corrupted from the simplicity that is in Christ. For
> if he that cometh preacheth another Jesus, whom
> we have not preached, or if ye receive another spirit,

which ye have not received, or another gospel, which ye have not accepted, ye might well bear with him. (2 Corinthians 11:3-4)

Consider that each time a wafer "Jesus" is "re-presented," as untold millions of Roman Catholics and Taizé followers believe, the true holy personage of Jesus of Nazareth is denigrated; His divine nature is lessened, His propitiatory blood-atoning substitutionary sacrifice on the Cross is undermined, and faith in Him *alone* for salvation becomes null and void. It was Christ Himself, in regard to His redemptive work on the Cross, who said, "It is finished" (i.e., the price for salvation has been "Paid in full").

Then saith he to [John] the disciple, Behold thy mother! And from that hour that disciple took her unto his own home. After this, Jesus knowing that all things were now accomplished, that the scripture might be fulfilled, saith, I thirst. Now there was set a vessel full of vinegar: and they filled a spunge with vinegar, and put it upon hyssop, and put it to his mouth. When Jesus therefore had received the vinegar, he said, It is finished: and he bowed his head, and gave up the ghost. (John 19:27-30)

JESUS IN HEAVEN VERSUS JESUS IN THE EUCHARIST

The global Catholic network (EWTN) and Father John A. Hardon, S. J. express these thoughts about the Eucharistic Christ:

Is there any real difference between Jesus in heaven and Jesus in the Eucharist? No, it is the same Jesus. The only difference is in us. We now on earth cannot see or touch him with our senses. But that is not a limitation in him; it is a limitation in us.

JESUS is really now on earth in the Eucharist.

Jesus IS really now on earth in the Eucharist.

Jesus is REALLY now on earth in the Eucharist.

Jesus is really NOW on earth in the Eucharist.

Jesus is really now ON earth in the Eucharist.

Jesus is really now on EARTH in the Eucharist.

Jesus is really now on earth IN THE EUCHARIST.

The foregoing six statements, repeated and separately emphasized, explain why the Catholic Church has defended the reality of the Real Presence so strenuously down the centuries.*[7]

Evangelical researcher and author Ray Yungen put it this way:

Everything vital in the Catholic Church springs from the Eucharist (communion). What is simply

---

*For more in-depth documentation on the error of the Eucharist, please read *Another Jesus* by Roger Oakland.

a component in the evangelical church is *the* major component in the Catholic Church. In fact, many Catholic works reference the Eucharist that it carries on the work of our redemption as in the following example from Father Robert J. Fox, in his book *The Catholic Faith*:

"Catholics are bound under pain of mortal sin to participate in the Sacrifice of the Mass every Sunday and holy day of obligation. Only a *serious* reason would excuse one. Inconvenience, laziness, company came, being tired, poor clothing, head-ache, etc. are *not* sufficient excuses."[8]

A SIMPLE QUESTION WITH PROFOUND IMPLICATIONS

One essential question must be asked, "How is one going to find Christian 'love,' 'peace,' 'unity,' and 'the gospel' in the Taizé Community when a practice is upheld there that re-crucifies the Christ who once and for all died for the sins of the world?" The book of Hebrews is very clear and succinct on this subject as if purposely written as a refutation of the Eucharist as a continual resacrificing of Christ:

[B]ut this man, after he had offered *one sacrifice* for sins *for ever*, sat down on the right hand of God . . . Now where remission of these is, there is *no more* offering for sin. (Hebrews 10:12, 18; also read Hebrews 9:23 to 10:18)

To take Jesus' one-time sacrifice on Calvary and repeat it again and again only cheapens and extinguishes the wonderful gift of forgiveness that Jesus accomplished when He said, "It is finished" (John 19:30).

Some Taizé brothers want to follow a Roman Catholic priesthood and pope and believe they are eating and in-gesting God who has been *mystically* invoked through the Eucharist. Other Taizé brothers don't agree with this but overlook it because they—as liberal Protestants—no longer protest the heresies of Rome and the blasphemy of "the Real Presence" in the Eucharist.

For many years, the Taizé Community has been pioneering a "Christian unity" that is not Christian at all. How does this happen? By marching arm-in-arm in the name of interfaith ecumenism while trampling biblical truth underfoot. Instead of preaching the biblical Gospel and interpreting Scripture from a literal, historical, and grammatical viewpoint, Taizé is leading multitudes into mystical experiences, which cause the overall spiritual outlook in the practitioner to transform into an interspiritual, *panentheistic* spirituality. Simply put, Scripture is not the standard, and herein lies the very root of the problem.

The Taizé Community holds to a no-holds-barred mentality. *Merriam Webster's Dictionary* defines "no-holds-barred" as being "without restrictions of hampering conven-tions" and "free from the usual limits or rules." The Taizé Community and similar, like-minded, interfaith groups choose to operate contrary to Scripture, "without restrictions of hampering [biblical discernment] conventions" and "free from the usual [scriptural/theological] limits or rules."

In laymen's terms, justification by faith alone means that through simple childlike faith in the Person and finished work of Jesus Christ on the Cross and His resurrection from the dead, one is declared perfectly righteous before the Almighty God, who created the heavens and the earth. As a result of Christ's death at Calvary, when He was made the "propitiatory sacrifice" for our sins, God's anger and just wrath against sin has been completely satisfied. Jesus, being our All Holy Substitute on the Cross, paid for our redemption with His own blood and resurrected from the dead three days later. Our sin (transgression against the Law of God) was dealt with completely at the Cross—the punishment that we deserve for sinning against God was put upon Christ instead of us. We, the guilty, go free because He, the Sinless Savior, bore our punishment to set us free. Born-again Christians are justified (declared righteous) before God based on what Jesus already did for sinful humanity, not through what a priest today does by blasphemously re-presenting (sacrificing) Christ in the Eucharist, *plus* one's good works. When a person truly believes in Jesus Christ and trusts in what He has done for him, then is he "made alive in Christ" (Ephesians 2:1-22) by God's Holy Spirit who comes to dwell in him and through him (Ephesians 3). Hence the term, "born-again" (John 3:3).

CATHOLIC VERSUS PROTESTANT BELIEFS ON SALVATION AND THE GOSPEL

[In 2014] the Pope declared a very Catholic understanding of salvation. According to the *Catholic News Service*, "Pope Francis described as 'dangerous' the temptation to believe that one can have 'a personal, direct, immediate relationship with Jesus Christ without communion with and the mediation of the church.'"[1]

M any leaders in the evangelical church today are saying that the differences between Roman Catholicism and Protestant Christianity are not significant enough to keep the two bodies separated in fellowship and vision. But is that an accurate assessment? If it is, then there is no harm in the efforts of Taizé to bring the two together. But if the differences *are* significant, and especially if those differences have to do with salvation and the Gospel message of Jesus Christ, then any efforts to unite the two must be brought to the light and scrutinized.

The late apologetics author John Weldon (d. 2014) wrote a clarification of the primary doctrinal differences between Protestants and Roman Catholics in his book (co-authored with John Ankerberg) *Protestants and Catholics: Do They Now Agree?* Weldon warns:

> The bottom line is this: It is virtually impossible to claim to maintain important doctrinal distinctions on the one hand and to simultaneously unite Catholic and Protestant believers into a spiritual fellowship on the other.[2]

Continuing, Weldon refutes the Roman Catholic doctrine of salvation by discussing several essential doctrines and how they relate to Catholic teaching:

> *Propitiation/atonement.* This doctrine demonstrates that the death of Christ fully propitiated or satisfied God's wrath and paid the full divine penalty for [sin] . . . thereby proving that neither the [Roman Catholic] sacraments, penance, purgatorial suffering, indulgences, the Mass, priests, nor any other aspect of the Catholic Church is involved in any way in the propitiation or remitting of sin.

> *Reconciliation.* This doctrine involves one result of the death of Christ for sin wherein the state of enmity between God and man is replaced by one of peace and fellowship, proving that final reconciliation between God and man is something accomplished by God on behalf of man, not by the [Roman Catholic] Church on behalf of man.

Justification. This doctrine constitutes the legal declaration of the believer's absolute righteousness before God on the basis of his personal faith in Jesus Christ, proving that our perfect standing before God is not dependent upon [Roman Catholic] Church teaching, sacraments, personal character, or good works, but solely upon our faith in Christ.

Sanctification. This doctrine involves being set apart to God for His glory. A correct understanding of its past, present, and future applications proves that sanctification does not lead to justification, nor should it be confused with regeneration, as [Roman] Catholicism teaches.[3]

It is sad to say, but it is true that Taizé Community members are willing victims of grave theological compromise. Their own personal collaboration and "fellowship" with those who use prayer as a platform to engage in ecumenical Christianity, repetitive praying/chanting, and contemplative spirituality, is unbiblical.

In addition to the biblical doctrines listed above and their contrast with Roman Catholic doctrine, the Catholic view of Mary, the mother of Jesus, cannot be overlooked. Pope John Paul II said this:

Mary is present with the Church and as the Mother of the Church, at each of our celebrations of the Eucharist. . . . Mary Most Holy, in whom the Eucharistic mystery shows itself more than in anyone else, as mystery of light.[4]

Apologist and author Roger Oakland explains the problem with this in his book, *Another Jesus: The Eucharistic Christ and the New Evangelization*:

> Think about the implications of this statement! According to the [former] head of the Catholic Church, when the ordained priest consecrates the wafer during Mass, not only does *Jesus* appear, but the *mother* of Jesus also shows up. Of course, this contradicts the Bible's affirmation that only God is omnipresent.[5]

Biblical Christian theology and Roman Catholic theology are at odds with each other in many ways, especially regarding the component parts of salvation. In fact, the attempt to create spiritual fellowship and unity between Roman Catholics, Protestants (regarded as the "lost" or "separated" brethren), Eastern Orthodox believers, Word Faith/prosperity-gospel adherents, and so on is not only wrong but dangerous. And this spiritual blending is happening all around the world as can be seen through the global rise in interfaith movements, New Age events, ecumenical festivals, the Spiritual Formation movement, the Purpose Driven movement, and the emerging church. Unfortunately, untold millions of people who think they are pursuing God are, in actuality, becoming entangled with our adversary, the devil, who is the father of lies and deceit.

TAIZÉ ENDORSED BY ECUMENISTS AND POPES ALIKE (AND EVEN SOME EVANGELICALS)

> [I]t is appropriate to speak briefly on the Second Vatican Council's initiative once more to set the Church on the path of ecumenism. This path is very dear to me. . . . [People] need to know which of these churches or communities [Protestant or Catholic] is that of Christ, since He founded only one Church—the only one capable of speaking in His name.[1]—Pope John Paul II

Sadly, many practitioners of the Taizé contemplative style of worship have subjected themselves to a movement which at the very core is steeped with serious theological contradictions. Regardless of one's religious background, including Roman Catholic, Protestant, and Eastern Orthodox, the Taizé Community has blended them all together in their worship services.

So that the reader is aware of the excess ecumenical nature and drastic blurring of theological distinctions surrounding the Taizé Community, several quotations are listed below from famous leaders. These quotes are from the Taizé website—from the "Celebration of the 70th anniversary of Taizé" page.

"THE BROTHERS" AT TAIZÉ, FRANCE

POPE BENEDICT XVI: In these days when we remember the return to the Father of dear Brother Roger, the founder of the Taizé Community . . . His Holiness Pope Benedict XVI wants you to know his spiritual closeness and union in prayer with the Community and all those involved in commemorating the memory of Brother Roger.

A tireless witness to the gospel of peace and reconciliation, Brother Roger was a pioneer in the difficult paths toward unity among the disciples of Christ. . . . Although he has entered eternal joy, he still speaks to us. May his witness to an ecumenism of holiness inspire us in our march towards unity, and may your Community continue to live and to radiate his charism, especially towards the younger generations!

With all his heart, the Holy Father asks God to fill you with his blessings, as well as the brothers of the Taizé Community and all who are involved with you on the roads to unity among the disciples of Christ, especially the young.

PATRIARCH BARTHOLOMEW OF CONSTANTINOPLE (EASTERN ORTHODOX): We want to send the prior, Brother Alois, and the entire Taizé Community these few words to commemorate the fifth anniversary of the tragic death of the late Brother Roger . . . He was not only its founder and inspiration, but also the "watchman," tireless and always available, at the bedside of its development, at the service of the powerful idea that founded it, what he called "ecumenical reconciliation."

PATRIARCH KYRILL OF MOSCOW (RUSSIAN ORTHODOX): Dear Brother Alois! Dear brothers and sisters in Christ! With all my heart I greet you, representatives of different peoples, countries and Christian churches, who are gathered today. . . . Today at Taizé a hundred brothers, Catholics and Protestants, live together. And the community is often visited by young believers from the Orthodox Churches. It seems important to me that young people be brought together on the basis of *the common heritage of the ancient Church*, which the community studies carefully and tries to follow.[2]

Many more quotes could be provided from ecumenical leaders endorsing the Taizé Community including the following notable ones: the former Archbishop of Canterbury, Rowan Williams, as well as General Secretary of the Lutheran World Federation, Ishmael Noko. Noko wrote:

> The [Taizé] community has given to Christians everywhere distinctive forms of chant that unite us as we sing. In this music the hope of the community, to be a means and foretaste of Christian unity, has found an unexpected expression.[3]

And congratulating the Taizé Community, the General Secretary of the World Communion of Reformed Churches, Setri Nyomi, states:

> We celebrate especially the impact that the Taizé Community has on hundreds of thousands of young people around the world.[4]

Olav Fykse-Tveit, the General Secretary of the World Council of Churches expresses his views of Taizé:

> On behalf of the World Council of Churches, a fellowship of 349 churches, I am honored to share our greetings on this solemn and special occasion to all the brothers arid [sic] sisters in the Taizé Community.
>
> The entire WCC fellowship of churches rejoices with you as you celebrate seventy years since the Taizé Community was founded by Brother Roger . . . The holistic mission of the Taizé community has touched

the lives of millions and yet, there is much work still ahead . . . The fellowship of WCC member churches, by God's grace, also stands alongside the Taizé community in celebration, thanksgiving and prayer.[5]

The Archbishop of York, John Sentamu (Church of England), concluded his commendation of the Taizé Community this way:

Seventy years of the Community has set a deep foundation of pilgrimage and trust. With all God's love and blessing.[6]

Also of note is the following statement showing the close friendship between Brother Roger and John Paul II when he was Pope. Brother Roger wrote, "John Paul II received me every year in private audience . . ."[7] Brother Roger also wrote of how he sought to assure "[John Paul II] of the trust our [Taizé] community had in him."[8]

On the Taizé website, an article titled "One Passes Through Taizé as One Passes Close to a Spring of Water," the closeness of Brother Roger and Pope John Paul II is again confirmed:

Brother Roger met Karol Wojtyla, the future Pope John Paul II, in 1962, during the Vatican Council, when he was still the young auxiliary Bishop of Krakow. As Archbishop of Krakow, Mgr Wojtyla visited Taizé twice, in 1964 and 1968.

After he became pope in 1978, he received Brother Roger every year in private audience. He welcomed in Rome the thousands of young adults of three of the end-of-the-year European meetings. During one of his journeys, the Pope visited Taizé in 1986.[9]

MANY CHURCH LEADERS AND REPRESENTATIVES OF OTHER RELIGIONS COME TOGETHER AT TAIZÉ

On August 16, 2015, many representatives of Christian and other religions were present at Taizé in memory of Brother Roger's passing. Here is the list from their website:

- Interdenominational Christian Organizations
- Catholic Church
- Orthodox Churches
- Oriental Orthodox Churches
- Old Catholic Church
- Protestant and Evangelical Churches[10]

Within each subheading on this web page, there is a lengthy list of names and titles representing each denomination. The "Protestant and Evangelical Churches" subheading alone includes a long list of churches under further sub-heading categories. These titles include— "Anglican Communion, Lutherans, Reformed, United Churches, Methodists, Baptists, Adventists, Salvation Army, Pentecostal Church, Full Gospel Church."

Below all of these listings is yet another main boldface heading and bullet list:

Representatives of Other Religions

- Hinduism
- Buddhism
- Judaism
- Islam[11]

Picture a whole Smörgåsbord of ecumenical Christians praying together with representatives from other world religions? Is this the God of the Bible to whom these from different religions are praying? How could it be? The apostle John writes:

> Little children, it is the last time: and as ye have heard that antichrist shall come, even now are there many antichrists; whereby we know that it is the last time. They went out from us, but they were not of us; for if they had been of us, they would no doubt have continued with us: but they went out, that they might be made manifest that they were not all of us. But ye have an unction from the Holy One, and ye know all things. (1 John 2:18-20)

Just as the Taizé Community has succumbed to the Roman Catholic fold (the popes), so, too, all ecumenically compromised Protestant denominations will eventually be assimilated as well. It is just a matter of time.

Before this book went to press, I did a search on the Internet to see which evangelical and mainline denominations were holding Taizé services in the United States and Canada. Here is a partial list:

Mennonite	Lutheran
Episcopal	Presbyterian
United Methodist	Wesleyan
Baptist	Congregational

A 2014 article in the *Baptist Standard* titled "Contemplative Weekend Draws Young People to Austin [Texas]" states:

> An ecumenical monastic community in France sponsored an event at a Texas Baptist church. . . . The Brothers of Taizé, who represent various Christian denominations and 25 countries, sponsored a "Pilgrimage of Trust" at First Baptist Church in Austin. . . . Christian families from varied churches in Austin opened their homes for overnight lodging and provided transportation for pilgrimage participants.[12]

Several evangelical colleges and seminaries are holding Taizé services as well.

Taizé practitioners, although perhaps well-meaning, are caught in the middle of a dangerous ecumenical vortex, a vortex that is a spiritual black hole masquerading as "a community where kindness of heart and simplicity would be at the centre of everything"[13] (Brother Roger). But it is most certainly not very kind and not very simple when the lines that make up the doctrine of salvation are so blurred and misconstrued.

Is it "loving" and "kind" and a great work of "hope and solidarity," to subject hopeful spiritual seekers and ministers from numerous world religions into a "prayerful" mixture and theological maze, where one is encouraged to pray together with advocates of pagan spirituality and unbiblical forms of Christianity—in the name of Christian brotherhood and sisterhood? This can only sow confusion.

Would a loving and kind father or mother withhold information or purposefully confuse their own children about when and how a child should cross the street or not warn them about the dangers of fire, or household chemicals, or the danger of drowning? It is amazing that so many millions of young people are gathering together to worship at the Taizé Community, and yet many of them have completely opposite understandings about God and what salvation is and is not. Ray Yungen reminds us of the true ministry of reconciliation:

> While God sent His Son, Jesus Christ, to die for the sins of the world, He did not say all would be saved. His words are clear that many would reject the salvation He provided. But those who are saved have been given the "ministry of reconciliation" (2 Corinthians 5:18) making an appeal to those who are perishing (2 Corinthians 4:3).[14]

Reconciliation and unity can only be found in the work and Person of Jesus Christ. Other religions would reject this. And the Roman Catholic Church, in essence, rejects it too because they teach *another* Jesus and *another* Gospel. "The Christian message is not . . . the contemplative silence. It is the power of the Cross!"[15]

> For the preaching of the cross is to them that perish foolishness; but unto us which are saved it is the power of God. (1 Corinthians 1:18)

71

A NARROW WAY OR
THE BROAD ROAD?

My motivation in writing this book is to convey in a loving and biblical way that God is the Spirit of truth (John 14:17; 16:13) and that He is not the author of confusion (1 Corinthians 14:33). All who would seek to know Him and to experience true Christian unity and prayer, according to Scripture, can only do so through the historical Jesus of Nazareth. A scriptural understanding of the doctrine of Christ and salvation can only be experienced by entering through the "narrow gate" that leads to everlasting life.

> Enter ye in at the strait gate: for wide is the gate, and broad is the way, that leadeth to destruction, and many there be which go in thereat: Because strait is the gate, and narrow is the way, which leadeth unto life, and few there be that find it. (Matthew 7:13-14)

That narrow gate that Jesus Christ is referring to is none other than Jesus Himself. He alone is Savior of the world.

If any Christian movement, church, or organization cannot stand upon what the Bible teaches about salvation, that movement, church, or organization should not even be considered as an option for Christian fellowship (Romans 16:17-18).

If believers in Jesus Christ desire to be unified in God's truth and to promote Christian prayer, they must recognize that Jesus Christ Himself is the "narrow" way that leads unto eternal life. The ecumenical, apostate, interfaith "broad" way—which will never provide the biblical message of salvation—is the broad road that leads to eternal destruction.

What do the Scriptures say regarding true Christian unity? If we have been "made alive in Christ" (born-again of God's Spirit), we have Christian unity. We are already unified through the Person and work of Jesus Christ and by His Holy Spirit who dwells in us. We are exhorted in Scripture in Ephesians to endeavor to "keep the unity of the Spirit in the bond of peace."

> I therefore, the prisoner of the Lord, beseech you that ye walk worthy of the vocation wherewith ye are called, With all lowliness and meekness, with longsuffering, forbearing one another in love; Endeavouring to keep the unity of the Spirit in the bond of peace. (Ephesians 4:1-3)

It is through the instruction of the Word of God and the sanctifying influence of the Holy Spirit in our lives that we are led to maturity in Christ—not through chanting and singing repetitive prayers and partaking in theologically confusing movements and practices.

The theology and teachings of the Taizé community and the Roman Catholic Church and popes that have helped move Taizé forward on earth are far removed indeed from the preaching and teaching of the early apostles and the sound teachings of Scripture. According to Scripture, God has given us "the word of reconciliation" and He "hath given to us the ministry of reconciliation." These are made known to us through the effective preaching and teaching of God's Gospel (Romans 1:1-5), not through differing and opposing "gospels" somehow blended together in a unified ecumenical community where the Gospel is not truly preached. Much damage has been done in the name of unity where the eternal destiny of precious souls is at stake. Thank God that Jesus Christ has provided for us in the Gospel, according to Scripture, not just a way but the only Way to eternal life.

If you have visited Taizé in France or have ever attended a Taizé service somewhere else, please consider the things you have read in this book. If you find you have questions, contact our ministry, and we will do our best to help. I cannot exhort you enough to study God's Word to see for yourself what is the whole counsel of God. And if you have been involved in any kind of mystical esoteric prayer practices that invoked spiritual experiences, even altered states of consciousness, I pray you will turn away from going in that direction, call upon the Lord in humble repentance, and ask Him to set you back on a straight path to Him. Remember the words of Jesus Christ:

> I am the way, the truth, and the life: no man cometh unto the Father, but by me. (John 14:16)

APPENDIX

THE DESERT FATHERS

BY RAY YUNGEN

Catholic priest William Shannon in his book, *Seeds of Peace*, explained the human dilemma as being the following:

> This forgetfulness, of our oneness with God, is not just a personal experience, it is the corporate experience of humanity. Indeed, this is one way to understanding original sin. We are in God, but we don't seem to know it. We are in paradise, but we don't realize it.[1]

Shannon's viewpoint defines the basic underlying worldview of the contemplative prayer movement as a whole. One can find similar quotations in practically every book written by contemplative authors. A Hindu guru or a Zen Buddhist master would offer the same explanation. This conclusion becomes completely logical when tracing the roots of contemplative prayer. Let us look at the beginnings of this practice.

In the early Middle Ages, there lived a group of hermits in the wilderness areas of the Middle East. They are known in history as the Desert Fathers. They dwelt in small isolated communities for the purpose of devoting their lives completely to God without distraction. The contemplative movement traces its roots back to these monks who promoted the mantra as a prayer tool. One meditation scholar made this connection when he said:

> The meditation practices and rules for living of these earliest Christian monks bear strong similarity to those of their Hindu and Buddhist renunciate brethren several kingdoms to the East . . . the meditative techniques they adopted for finding their God suggests either a borrowing from the East or a spontaneous rediscovery.[2]

Many of the Desert Fathers, in their zeal, were simply seeking God through trial and error. A leading contemplative prayer teacher candidly acknowledged the haphazard way the Desert Fathers acquired their practices:

> It was a time of great experimentation with spiritual methods. Many different kinds of disciplines were tried, some of which are too harsh or extreme for people today. Many different methods of prayer were created and explored by them.[3]

Attempting to reach God through occult mystical practices will guarantee disaster. The Desert Fathers of Egypt were located in a particularly dangerous locale at that time to be groping around for innovative approaches to God, because as one theologian pointed out:

> [D]evelopment of Christian meditative disciplines should have begun in Egypt because much of the intellectual, philosophical, and theological

basis of the practice of meditation in Christianity also comes out of the theology of Hellenic and Roman Egypt. This is significant because it was in Alexandria that Christian theology had the most contact with the various Gnostic speculations which, according to many scholars, have their roots in the East, possibly in India.[4]

Consequently, the Desert Fathers believed as long as the desire for God was sincere—anything could be utilized to reach God. If a method worked for the Hindus to reach their gods, then Christian mantras could be used to reach Jesus. A current practitioner and promoter of the Desert Fathers' mystical prayer still echoes the logical formulations of his mystical ancestors:

> In the wider ecumenism of the Spirit being opened for us today, we need to humbly accept the learnings of particular Eastern religions . . . What makes a particular practice Christian is not its source, but its intent . . . this is important to remember in the face of those Christians who would try to impoverish our spiritual resources by too narrowly defining them. If we view the human family as one in God's spirit, then this historical cross-fertilization is not surprising . . . selective attention to Eastern spiritual practices can be of great assistance to a fully embodied Christian life.[5]

Do you catch the reasoning here? Non-Christian sources, as avenues to spiritual growth, are perfectly legitimate in the Christian life, and if Christians only practice

TAIZÉ

their Christianity based on the Bible, they will actually impoverish their spirituality. This was the thinking of the Desert Fathers. So, as a result, we now have contemplative prayer. Jesus addressed this when he warned His disciples: "But when ye pray, use not vain repetitions, as the heathen do" (Matthew 6:7).

It should be apparent that mantra meditation or sacred word prayer qualifies as "vain repetition" and clearly fits an accurate description of the point Jesus was making. Yet in spite of this, trusted evangelical Christians have often pronounced that Christian mysticism is different from other forms of mysticism (such as Eastern or occult) because it is focused on Jesus Christ.

This logic may sound credible on the surface, but Christians must ask themselves a very simple and fundamental question: What really makes a practice Christian? The answer is obvious—does the New Testament sanction it? Hasn't Christ taught us, through His Word, to pray in faith in His name and according to His will? Did He leave something out? Would Jesus hold out on His true followers? Never!

Understanding this truth, God has declared in His Word that He does not leave it up to earnest, yet sinful people, to reinvent their own Christianity. When Christians ignore God's instructions in following Him, they end up learning the way of the heathen. Israel did this countless times. It is just human nature.

The account of Cain and Abel is a classic biblical example of spiritual infidelity. Both of Adam's sons wanted to please God, but Cain decided he would experiment with his own method of being devout. Cain must have reasoned

79

to himself: "Perhaps God would like fruit or grain better than a dead animal. It's not as gross. It's less smelly. Hey, I think I will try it!"

As you know, God was not the least bit impressed by Cain's attempt to create his own approach to pleasing God. The Lord made it clear to Cain that God's favor would be upon him if he did what was right, not just what was intended for God or "God-focused."

In many ways, the Desert Fathers were like Cain—eager to please but not willing to listen to the instruction of the Lord and do what is right. One cannot fault them for their devotion, but one certainly can fault them for their lack of discernment.

ENDNOTES

Chapter 1: A Community in the Mountains of France

1. The Beginnings, http://www.taize.fr/en_article6526.html.

2. The Beginnings, op. cit.

3. William Madges and Michael Daley (editors), *Vatican II: 50 Person Stories* (Orbis Books, 2012), p. 175.

Chapter 2: Reconciliation—A Theological Theme at Taizé

1. Jason Brian Santos, *A Community Called Taizé: A Story of Prayer, Worship and Reconciliation* (IVP Books, 2008, Kindle Edition), Kindle Location 1366.

2. Ibid.

3. Rob Baker and Gray Henry, Editors, *Merton and Sufism* (Louisville, KY: Fons Vitae, 1999), pp. 109-110.

4. Ibid.

5. Jason Brian Santos, op. cit.,

6. http://www.webster-dictionary.org/definition/Reconciliation.

7. Roger Oakland, *The Good Shepherd Calls: An Urgent Message to the Last-Days Church* (Eureka, MT: Lighthouse Trails Publishing, Inc, 2017), p. 131.

8. "Why have millions of young people visited an ecumenical monastic community in France?" (InterVarsity Press website: https://web-beta.archive.org/web/20100104080925/https://www.ivpress.com/title/ata/3525-look.pdf).

Chapter 3: The Taizé Community in Ecumenical Overdrive

1. Keynote address by Dr. Samuel Kobia, General Secretary World Council of Churches, Challenges Facing the Ecumenical

Movement in the 21st Century, Interchurch Center, New York, Oct 22, 2005, https://www.oikoumene.org/en/resources/documents/wcc-programmes/ecumenical-movement-in-the-21st-century/foundational-texts/challenges-facing-the-ecumenical-movement-in-the-21st-century.

2. From the World Council of Churches website: http://www.oikoumene.org/en/resources/logo.

3. Keynote address by Dr. Samuel Kobia, op. cit.

4. Ibid.

5. Ibid.

6. Ibid.

7. Ibid.

8. Ibid.

9. Dr. Samuel Kobia, "Acceptance of Election as General Secretary" (World Council of Churches, August 28, 2003, http://www.oikoumene.org/en/resources/documents/general-secretary/speeches/acceptance-of-election-as-general-secretary).

10. Ecumene, Modernity, Religion (https://en.wikipedia.org/wiki/Ecumene).

11. Robert Wilson-Black, "Denying Christ and Getting to the Truth—Lessons From a Week at Taizé" (Sojourners website, August 27, 2015, https://sojo.net/articles/denying-christ-and-getting-truth).

12. "The Community Today" (http://www.taize.fr/en_article6525.html.)

13. "Interview with Cardinal Kasper Three Years After the Death of Brother Roger" (EWTN Catholic Network, taken from: *L'Osservatore Romano,* Weekly Edition in English, August 27, 2008, http://www.ewtn.com/library/CHRIST/kasproger.htm,), p. 13.

14. Ibid.

Chapter 4: A Life Long Commitment to Celibacy

1. "A Life Long Commitment" (http://www.taize.fr/en_article6.html).

2. Mike Oppenheimer, "Marriage and the Priesthood" (http://

www.letusreason.org/rc20.htm).

3. Australian Government's Royal Commission on Child Abuse (see several documents regarding Frank Houston's sexual abuse activities: http://childabuseroyalcommission.gov.au/search?-searchtext=frank+houston+&searchmode=anyword).

Chapter 5: "God Lives Within Every Human Being"

1. Brother Alois, "A Pilgrimage of Trust" (http://www.taize.fr/en_article58.html).

2. Brother Roger, *God is Love Alone* (Chicago, IL: GIA Publications, original French version 2001, 2003), p. 16.

3. *Catechism of the Catholic Church* (New York, NY: Doubleday, 1994), p. 228.

4. Ibid., p. 129. (These two quotes are courtesy of Warren B. Smith from his book, *"Another Jesus" Calling: How Sarah Young's False Christ is Deceiving the Church,* 2nd edition, Mountain Stream Press, 2016.)

5. Brother Roger, *God is Love Alone,* op. cit., p. 16.

6. Neale Donald Walsch, *Conversations with God: an uncommon dialogue,* Book 2 (Charlottesville, VA: Hampton Roads, 1997), p. 35.

7. Ibid., p. 56.

8. Warren B. Smith, *Be Still and Know That You are Not God!* *(Eureka, MT: Lighthouse Trails Publishing, 2015), p. 3.*

Chapter 6: Taizé Worship

1. The Cornilo Churches, UK (http://www.cornilochurches.org.uk/taiz.htm).

2. The Contemplative Network, "Prayer With the Songs of Taizé (http://www.contemplative.net/prayer-with-songs-taize-t-1_43.html).

3. "Inside the Taizé Community: An Interview with Brother Emile" (http://www.asacredjourney.net/2013/08/taize).

Chapter 8: Taizé and the Eucharist—An Interspiritual Hybrid

1. Brother Alois, Letter from Cochabamba (Taizé Community website; At the Wellspring of Faith, http://www.taize.fr/en_rubrique12.html).

2. Brother Roger, *The Rule of Taizé* (London, UK: SPCK Publishing, 2012, original French version copyright 1954), p. 11.

3. John A. Hardon, S. J. "Holy Eucharist is the Whole Christ" (*Soul Magazine*. Published by the World Apostolate of Fatima; Blue Army, Washington, NJ., https://www.ewtn.com/faith/teachings/eucha5.htm, posted on the EWTN website).

4. J.C. Ryle, "Why Were Our Reformers Burned?" (Hertfordshire, England: Evangelical Press, from *Light from Old Times,* 1890, First Evangelical Press Press edition, 1980), pp. 15-55.

5. John A. Hardon, S.J., "Holy Eucharist is the Whole Christ," op. cit.

6. Ibid.

7. Ibid.

8. Ray Yungen, *Simple Answers: Understanding the Catholic Faith—An Evangelical Primer* (Eureka, MT: Lighthouse Trails Publishing, Inc, 2017), chapter 3, citing Father Robert J. Fox, in his book *The Catholic Faith,* p. 269.

Chapter 9: Catholic Versus Protestant Beliefs on Salvation and the Gospel

1. Cindy Wooden, "Church is Essential for Faith; There are no 'Free Agents,' Pope Says" (*Catholic News Service,* June 25, 2014, https://www.ncronline.org/blogs/francis-chronicles/church-essential-faith-there-are-no-free-agents-pope-says).

2. John Ankerberg and John Weldon, *Protestants and Catholics: Do They Now Agree* (Eugene, OR: Harvest House Publishers, 1995), p. 270.

3. Ibid., pp. 270-271.

4. "Mary Has a Place in Latest Encyclical" (*Zenit,* April 17, 2003, https://zenit.org/articles/mary-has-a-place-in-latest-encyclical).

5. Roger Oakland, *Another Jesus: The Eucharistic Christ and the New Evangelization* (Eureka, MT: Lighthouse Trails Publishing, Inc, 2007 Edition), p. 115.

Chapter 10: Taizé Endorsed by Ecumenists and Popes Alike (And Even Some Evangelicals)

1. John Paul II, *Crossing the Threshold of Hope* (New York, NY: Alfred A. Knopf, 1994), pp. 144-146.

2. http://www.taize.fr/en_article11121.html.

3. Ibid.

4. Ibid.

5. Ibid.

6. Ibid.

7. "One passes through Taizé as one passes close to a spring of water" (http://www.taize.fr/en_article6718.html).

8. Ibid.

9. Ibid.

10. Many Church Leaders and Representatives of Other Religions at Taizé (http://www.taize.fr/en_article19326.html).

11. Ibid.

12. Daniel Wallace, "Contemplative Weekend Draws Young People to Austin" (*Baptist Standard*, April 5, 2014, https://www.baptiststandard.com/news/texas/16310-contemplative-weekend-draws-young-people-to-austin-church).

13. Community (http://www.taize.fr/en_rubrique8.html).

14. Ray Yungen, *A Time of Departing* (Eureka, MT: Lighthouse Trails Publishing, Inc, 2006, 2nd edition), p. 52.

15. Ibid.

Appendix: The Desert Fathers

1. William Shannon, *Seeds of Peace* (New York, NY: Crossroad Publishing, 1996), p. 66.

2. Daniel Goleman, *The Meditative Mind* (Los Angeles, CA: Tarcher/Putnam Inc., 1988), p.53.

3. Ken Kaisch, *Finding God: A Handbook of Christian Meditation*

(Mahwah, NJ: Paulist Press, 1994), p.191.

4. Father William Teska, *Meditation in Christianity* (Himalayan Institute, 1973), p.65.

5. Tilden Edwards, *Living in the Presence* (San Francisco, CA: Harper & Row, 1987), Acknowledgment page.

PHOTO CREDITS

Cover: From Fotosearch.com; used with permission; old church in Taizé, France.

Page 12: From Creative Commons; photo taken by Steffen Banhardt; used with permission.

Page 16: From Wikimedia Commons; copyright owner: Dietrich Benninghaus, Germany; used with permission.

Page 20: From Wikipedia; copyright owner: Wolfgang H. Wögerer, Vienna, Austria; used with permission.

Page 30: From Alamy.com; used with permission.

Page 38: From Wikimedia Commons; copyright owner: Damir Jelic; used with permission.

Page 64: From Creative Commons; photo taken by Maciej Biłas; used with permission.

Page 72: From bigstockphoto.com; used with permission.

THE
GOOD SHEPHERD
CALLS

BY ROGER OAKLAND

SINCE THE TURN of the
millennium, in particular
since September 11, 2001
when America was attacked
by terrorists triggering a global-wide spiritual paradigm
shift, Christianity as we have known it has experienced
a major meltdown. While many are saying Christianity
is on the brink of a great revival and even a "new
reformation," in reality, we are witnessing the greatest
apostasy in modern-day history.

The Good Shepherd Calls brings clarity to what this
delusion looks like, why it is happening, where it is
headed, and what can still be done to warn believers
and unbelievers alike.

Released 2017 by Lighthouse Trails | $14.95 | 288 pages

To Order Additional copies of:

TAIZÉ

send $10.95 plus $3.25 for shipping to:
Lighthouse Trails Publishing
P.O. Box 908
Eureka, Montana 59917

Call or go online for information about quantity discounts.
You may order online at
www.lighthousetrails.com
or
Call our toll free number:
866/876-3910
[ORDER LINE—USA & CANADA]

For international orders and all other calls: 406/889-3610.
You may also mail or fax your order. Our fax line is 406/889-3633.
You can print an order form from our website if you prefer.

Taizé, as well as all books by Lighthouse Trails Publishing, can be ordered
directly from Lighthouse Trails or through all major outlet stores,
bookstores, online bookstores and Christian bookstores.

Bookstores may order through Ingram, Spring Arbor, Anchor, or
directly from Lighthouse Trails. Libraries may order through
Baker and Taylor or Lighthouse Trails. Quantity discounts
available for most of our books.
Also check out our website for special international ordering
through one of our international distributors.
For more information: Lighthouse Trails Research Project
www.lighthousetrailsresearch.com or www.lighthousetrails.com

YOU MAY VISIT THE AUTHOR'S WEBSITE AT:
WWW.SPIRITUAL-RESEARCH-NETWORK.COM

Printed in Great Britain
by Amazon

48216961R00052